Table of Contents

Introduction

Have you ever been snorkeling in the Bahamas or Hawaii? If you have, you probably saw colorful fish and stunning corals. What if you could have a chunk of that in your bedroom, how cool would that be? In The Beginner's Guide to Saltwater Aquariums, we will cover everything you need to know about setting up and taking care of your little ocean!

Taking care of and setting up a saltwater aquarium can be hard and confusing because there are lots of varying opinions. However, if you read this book, you can easily set up your fish tank with no tears. Note: This book only covers fish and Invertebrates that can live in a 20-gallon aquarium.

Equipment and Setup

When starting the saltwater fish tank as a hobby, start small (20 gallons and under). The reason to start small is so you can learn what equipment you need and how to use it, before moving on to expensive and complicated equipment. This will also be an inexpensive and easy setup for under $500.

Necessary Equipment

Tank

First, you would need a fish tank. I would recommend a 20-gallon to start with because you can have a variety of creatures living in it, and it is easy to maintain.

$20-40

Heater

You must have your water at least 78 to 82 degrees Fahrenheit. Ensure to buy a heater that automatically turns off and can maintain a specific temperature perfectly, because if fish or corals are in cold or hot water for too long, they will die.

$15-30

Rocks and sand

Rocks in your fish tank will look awesome and are a good place to stick corals. When starting a saltwater fish tank use live sand because it has beneficial bacteria which will help your fish tank thrive. You will need 1-2 inches of sand in your tank.

$50-60

Stand

Then to hold your tank, you need a stand. Your stand needs to be able to hold 500 pounds. Water is VERY heavy.

$100-300

Filter

The filter is one of the most important pieces of equipment in any fish tank. It helps clean your water and hosts a place for beneficial bacteria to live and grow. When buying a filter for a saltwater aquarium, I would recommend multiplying the size of your tank times 3 to get your filter. For example, for a 20-gallon tank, you need to multiply by 3, (20x3=60) so you will need a 60-gallon filter.

$10-50

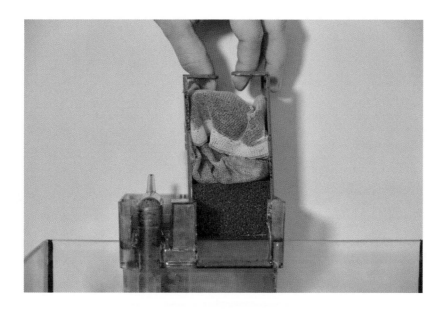

Circulation Pump/Wavemaker

To mimic the tides and water movement you will need a wavemaker or circulation pump. This will help blow debris off rocks, sand, and corals. It will stop the rotting of food, so you don't have random gunk in your tank.

$ 10-15

Lighting

Lights will help make your fish tank look amazing. Blue and Purple UV lights can also help to grow coral.

$50-100

Thermometer

The thermometer helps measure the water's temperature. It is handy because if you figure out your heater is defective you can save your pets.

$3-5

Refractometer/Hydrometer

These tools will help you monitor the salinity and gravity in your tank.

Salt mixture

Most Pet stores sell salt for saltwater fish tanks this is what makes the tank saltwater.

Lid

If you plan on getting jumping fish, you will need to get a lid to keep the fish from jumping out.

Setting up your tank

1. Start by pouring the sand into your tank

2. Then place your rocks inside the tank

3. To mix the saltwater, get a bucket and pour dechlorinated water. Then pour the right amount of salt into the bucket. Put your circulation pump into the bucket

4. Let it sit for ten minutes and pour it into the tank

5. Repeat steps 3 and 4 until the tank fills

6. Place the Filter, Heater, circulation pump, and thermometer into the tank

7. Use your Refractometer or hydrometer and test your salinity. Aim for 35 or 36

8. If the salinity is too high, take out some saltwater and replace it with dechlorinated water. If salinity is low add more salt. Do this until the salinity is perfect. Note: NEVER add salt to a tank that has fish or coral in it

9. Add live beneficial Bacteria to the Tank

10. Let the Tank sit for about a week

11. Add cycle-safe fish (described in the next chapter)

Fish

Now that you have set your tank up it is time for fish. You must be careful because if not chosen carefully fish can end up fighting with others, which usually ends in disaster. You will also want to stick to the thumb rule which is 1 gallon of water for every inch of the fish. Make sure you float your fish over the water for 30 minutes, so they can accumulate to new water temperatures.

Need to know

😁　- This means this is a peaceful fish that can live with other peaceful fish

😠　- This means semi-aggressive they can co-exist with semi-aggressive fish

😡　- Very aggressive they will attack and kill peaceful fish, and can only be kept with very aggressive fish

🦘　- This means the fish will jump, they require a lid

🧍　- This means that this fish will not jump, but in bad water conditions they will jump

👍　- This means this fish can live with coral

👎　- This fish cannot live with coral

🦀　- This means this fish can live with crabs and snails

🚫　- This means this fish cannot live with crabs and snails

Chromis

Chromis are amazing, hardy, reef-safe, peaceful, and cycle-safe fish. Overall they are the best beginner fish. These fish like to school so you will need at least 4. They only grow up to 3 inches so you can have a small school in a 15-gallon tank. There are also many types of Chromis like Blue-Green, Blue, and Black Bar Chromis. They are also relatively inexpensive; they can range from $10-30.

Clownfish

The clownfish are also known as anemonefish. This is a popular fish because of the film Finding Nemo. This fish is perfect for beginners. They are also very Hardy fish which makes them cycle-safe. They are also inexpensive ranging from $15-30. There are also many types of clownfish such as Mocha, Ocellaris, Percula, and Blizzard. The most common type is the Ocellaris because it closely resembles Nemo and Marlin and is also inexpensive. There has been success in breeding clownfish in captivity but it is very hard. These fish can live with anemones except for condylactis. After clownfish are immune to the anemone's venom they will not go very far from it so a pair can live in a 10-gallon fish tank without space problems. These fish grow up to 3 inches and can live up to 10 years. The fish will eat flakes, pellets, and frozen foods.

Wrasse

😁/😣/😠
🦘
🦀/🚫
👍

Some species of wrasse are reef safe but some are not. Many types of reef-safe wrasse will not bother crabs and snails, but some species such as the six-line wrasse will pick on them until they die. Six-Line wrasse is also semi-aggressive. Most species are Reef-Safe wrasse such as the Bluehead fairy, Bluestreak cleaner, Exquisite fairy, Mcosker's flasher, and Ornate (shown above) wrasse are all peaceful and are good for beginners.

However, some wrasses can get very aggressive so you will have to do a lot of research before getting a wrasse. Many reef-safe wrasses are carnivores so they will need frozen food that has meat in it or flaked foods. Many wrasses get big growing up to 5 inches.

These fish can get expensive ranging from $20-150.

Gobies

Gobies are small and cute fish that grow up to only 2 inches. The most common species are the Firefish Goby (shown above) and Watchman Gobies. Watchman gobies will like to burrow in sand and hide in rocks. so make sure you have lots of hiding spots for them. Gobies are carnivores so you will need to buy frozen food or flaked foods.

Dottybacks

Dottybacks are amazing fish. They are hardy and very cute.

Dottybacks are semi-aggressive and will pick on other fish. They are

carnivores so they will need to eat frozen or flaked foods. They are

also reef safe and will not damage corals. The Best species to get

are the Bicolor, yellow, and Splendid dottybacks. They can get

pretty expensive ranging from $25-50. They are also small fish

ranging from 2 inches to 5 inches.

Cardinalfish

The Cardinal fish family is a small but amazing group of fish. The most common Cardinal fish are Banggai Cardinalfish (shown above) and the Pajama Cardinalfish. These fish are very small growing up to 2 inches. These fish are easy to breed in captivity. These fish have to be kept in small groups ranging from 2-4 fish.

These fish are slow swimmers so if aggressive fish are in the tank they will easily be attacked. These fish need lots of hiding spots because they are shy. Cardinalfish will meet up near long-spined sea urchins so if you cannot find your fish you may want to look there. They are also carnivores. Their price can range from $20-30.

Damsels

Damselfish are very aggressive and do not do well with other fish. They will stress other fish out. However, they are Hardy and Cycle-Safe. Their Aggression can be dealt with easily using the pasta strainer method (described in a later chapter). They have a very low price ranging from $10-20. The most commonly bought species are yellowtail, 3 striped, and azure (shown above) damsels. These fish will eat a variety of foods like flakes and pellets.

Basslets

Basslets love complicated rockwork to hide, so make sure to keep lots of hiding spots for them. They also like dim lighting. They are carnivores, so they will need frozen or live food to eat. Basslets are aggressive to their kind so only keep one in a tank. The best Basslet to get is the Royal Gramma Basslet. The Royal Gramma Basslet is very beautiful with half purple and half yellow.

Corals

Corals are amazing and beautiful animals and can come in a variety of different colors and shapes. In this book, I am going to cover the top 5 beginner corals. These corals are easy to maintain, fast-growing, and overall beautiful.

Before moving to corals I would start with a fish only with Live rock tank (FOWLER) and gradually level up to a reef tank. The best thing is that corals can live during the cycling process.

Zoanthids

Zoanthids are probably the best beginner coral because they can tolerate a lot of different lights and temperatures. They also grow VERY fast so if you don't want a ton of the same color zoanthid you will want to put them in a little rock island also known as a zoanthid garden. They are also gorgeous and look like little flowers. If you have a Zoanthid garden it will look like a little flower garden. Some types of zoanthids are toxic so do lots of research before getting one.

Mushroom Coral

The second most easy coral to take care of is Mushroom Coral just like zoanthids they grow like weeds and if not maintained and controlled they will take over your tank. Just like Zoanthids, you will want to keep them on a separate rock.

Birds Nest Coral

Birds nest Corals are also a common species for beginners just like Mushroom Corals And Zoanthids they grow fast. They are also colorful and inexpensive. The problem is when you place small frags you might want to keep the water flow low because the branches could easily snap. Howeve, you can raise the water flow when they grow bigger and stronger.

Palythoas

They are a Hardy and great beginner coral and come in a variety of colors however most palythoas are bland in color. They will look incredibly awesome next to Zoanthids and other Palythoas. Before buying Palythoas make sure to handle them with caution because they may obtain palytoxins which may kill you.

Green Star Polyps

These corals look like a wheat field on a windy day if your water flow is high. However, these corals also will grow rapidly so you will have to keep them isolated on a rock. You can also place them on the wall of your tank, and they will gladly cover the wall and you will have a coral background !

Coral Placement

First, figure out your coral's requirements (Lighting and water flow). Wherever you get your coral make sure to dip it, this is how to dip a coral:

- Get a bucket of fresh saltwater
- Accumulate the coral to the saltwater
- Place the coral in the bucket and have a drip accumulation going on
- Pour the needed amount of coral dip and use a circulation pump to have a good water flow
- Wait for 5 minutes
- Then place your coral in a place that would be ideal for it inside the tank. For example: if my coral needed high water flow and high lighting, I would place it closer to the top of the tank and next to the circulation pump
- To place your coral, take coral glue or epoxy and put it underneath your coral. So, the coral will stick onto the rock
- Place your coral

Food and feeding

Now you must feed your fish, this can be hard because you will need to feed the right amount of food, or else ammonia levels can rise, or your fish can starve. You will also want to feed the right food.

Feeding

Every day feed your fish once. Only feed each fish a little bit of food. Make sure every fish gets food. To feed corals use a syringe or dropper and drop the food into its mouth.

Coral Food

Roids

The most common food for coral is reef roids. This is a powdery food that you will need to mix with water before feeding your coral.

Zooplankton

Zooplankton is good food for both the coral and your fish. This can be bought in bottles or sometimes comes for free in live rock.

Fish Food

Flakes

It is the most common type of food for fish, it is usually inexpensive and contains foods that are perfect for the whole tank. Most flakes have food for both carnivores and herbivores.

Pellets

Just like Flakes, pellets are inexpensive and contain food for the whole tank.

Live Foods

Some carnivorous fish that are caught in the wild cannot eat flakes or pellets at first. They can be trained to eat flaked and pelleted foods but you will need to start with live foods. Foods such as brine shrimp, copepods, phytoplankton, and zooplankton are good live foods. These foods can be bought in bottles or you can hatch them in hatchery kits.

Frozen

Another common option is frozen food. Most frozen foods are for carnivores and herbivores so they can feed the whole tank. These foods should be kept in the freezer hence they are frozen.

Maintenance

Nice! You have set your tank up and have fish in it now it is time for maintenance. It is not very fun but it has to be done.

Daily Maintenance

- Feed the fish
- Scrape salt off the lights, filter, heater and stand
- Replace the evaporated water with fresh water and mix the scraped salt into it
- Monitor the salinity and gravity
- Monitor the temperature

Weekly Maintenance

- Feed corals using a Syringe or dropper and aim for the center where the mouth usually is
- Scrape Algae off the glass of your tank
- Do a 10% water change and replace it with new saltwater

Monthly Maintenance

For Monthly maintenance do another 10% water change, but this time use a gravel siphon and siphon the sand.

Common Problems

Once you have fish and coral in your tank you are going to face some problems such as algae growth, aggression, diseases, and cloudy water.

Algae Growth

Almost all beginners fear algae growing. Algae will not harm your fish and coral but will make your tank look ugly! Algae is easy to deal with. It can be scraped off with algae scrapers, magnets, and toothbrushes. You can also use algae-cleaning invertebrates like Trochus snails, Nassarius Snails, and Hermit Crabs.

Diatom

Just like algae Diatom will not affect your fish, but it will make your tank look bad. Diatom may look like algae, but it is different. If there is red algae-like stuff growing and spreading rapidly on your rocks, sand, and glass it is probably Diatom. Diatom most commonly grows at the beginning of most saltwater tanks, when the water parameters are unstable. Diatom is also the easiest problem to deal with. If you just leave it alone and continue with maintenance, it will die and your fish will probably eat it. However, hermit crabs like the blue-legged Hermit Crab and snails will eat Diatom which makes them go away faster.

Diseases

Just like humans, fish can get sick, also like humans some stores sell medicine for fish.

This is only for some beginners but having a quarantine tank will greatly help your fish. Just so you know what to look out for. Here are the most common diseases for saltwater fish.

Fin-Rot

Fin Rot is super easy to identify. If you look at your fish and its fins are disintegrated and shrinking your fish has fin-rot. This is usually caused by bad water quality and damage to the fins. First, check if there are sharp decorations in your tank that might harm your fish. Then do a water check and see if anything is weird. Treating this is easy, all you must do is do some 50% water changes because fin rot is usually from bad water quality. You can also try some medications from your pet store.

Constipation

Constipation is mostly caused by overfeeding or unhealthy diets. Symptoms are a swollen abdomen, lack of appetite, and resting at the bottom of the tank. This can easily be treated with Epsom salts (for fish) and medications from the pet store.

Pop-Eye

One day you look at your fish tank and see that one of your fish's eyes is sticking out of its eyes! This is the Pop-eye disease. This is caused by poor water quality and sometimes parasite infection (which is uncurable). More water changes may help the fish cure.

Swim Bladder Disease

You will know if your fish has this Disease, it is when your fish is swimming upside down and unbalanced while swimming. This usually happens during handling or fights when the swim bladder is injured. Sometimes it is bad water quality. This can be treated with antibiotics and water changes.

White Spot (Ich)

If you look closely at your fish you may see small white spots that are Ich. This is usually caused by a parasite infection. This can be treated with medicines that can be bought at your local pet store.

Aggression

Sometimes fish can get naughty and attack other fish, but aggression is easy to deal with the problem. This can be a problem especially when you are introducing new fish.

The Pasta Strainer Method

Did you know that fish can also get time-outs? That is exactly what the pasta strainer method does all you have to do is place the strainer on top of the tank and let the bully sit in it for 5 hours, making sure it is half submerged. Then the problem should be resolved, if not repeat the process until the fish learns its lesson.

Overfeeding

Fish love to eat sometimes they will get aggressive when it comes to food. To make sure every fish is getting food, sprinkling some extra flakes won't hurt.

Outro

Right now, you have all the information you need to set up your saltwater aquarium and care for your pets. The saltwater fish hobby is challenging and takes a lot of hard work. However, the result is always worth it! most people like to avoid Saltwater fish, however, these fish can be way more colorful and more eye-catching. Plus, Corals will make any house look 1,000 times better. Hopefully, you will be able to set up your saltwater tank. Good Luck Hobbyists!

Printed in Great Britain
by Amazon

38019329R00023